PENGUIN BOOKS

THE APOTHECARY'S HEIR

JULIANNE BUCHSBAUM earned an MFA from the Iowa Writers' Workshop and a PhD in literature from the University of Missouri. She is the author of *Slowly, Slowly, Horses* (2001) and *A Little Night Comes* (2005). Her poems have appeared in various journals, including *Conduit, Verse, Southwest Review,* and *Harvard Review*. She lives and works in Lawrence, Kansas.

THE NATIONAL POETRY SERIES

The National Poetry Series was established in 1978 to ensure the publication of five poetry books annually through five participating publishers. Publication is funded by the Lannan Foundation; Stephen Graham; Joyce & Seward Johnson Foundation; Juliet Lea Hillman Simonds; The Poetry Foundation; Olafur Olafsson; Mr.& Mrs. Michael Newhouse; Jennifer Rubell; The New York Community Trust; Elizabeth Christopherson; and Aristides Georgantas.

2011 Competition Winners

The Apothecary's Heir, by Julianne Buchsbaum of Lawrence, KS
Chosen by Lucie Brock-Broido, to be published by Penguin Books

Your Invitation to a Modest Breakfast, by Hannah Gamble of Chicago, IL
Chosen by Bernadette Mayer, to be published by Fence Books

Green Is for World, by Juliana Leslie of Santa Cruz, CA
Chosen by Ange Mlinko, to be published by Coffee House Press

Exit, Civilian, by Idra Novey of Brooklyn, NY
Chosen by Patricia Smith, to be published by University of Georgia Press

Maybe the Saddest Thing, by Marcus Wicker of Ann Arbor, MI
Chosen by D.A. Powell, to be published by HarperCollins Publishers

THE *A*POTHECARY'S *H*EIR

JULIANNE BUCHSBAUM

PENGUIN BOOKS

PENGUIN BOOKS
Published by the Penguin Group
Penguin Group (USA) Inc., 375 Hudson Street, New York, New York 10014, U.S.A.
Penguin Group (Canada), 90 Eglinton Avenue East, Suite 700, Toronto, Ontario,
Canada M4P 2Y3 (a division of Pearson Penguin Canada Inc.)
Penguin Books Ltd, 80 Strand, London WC2R 0RL, England
Penguin Ireland, 25 St Stephen's Green, Dublin 2, Ireland (a division of Penguin Books Ltd)
Penguin Group (Australia), 250 Camberwell Road, Camberwell, Victoria 3124,
Australia (a division of Pearson Australia Group Pty Ltd)
Penguin Books India Pvt Ltd, 11 Community Centre, Panchsheel Park,
New Delhi - 110 017, India
Penguin Group (NZ), 67 Apollo Drive, Rosedale, Auckland 0632,
New Zealand (a division of Pearson New Zealand Ltd)
Penguin Books (South Africa) (Pty) Ltd, 24 Sturdee Avenue, Rosebank,
Johannesburg 2196, South Africa

Penguin Books Ltd, Registered Offices:
80 Strand, London WC2R 0RL, England

First published in Penguin Books 2012

10 9 8 7 6 5 4 3 2 1

Page vii constitutes an extension of this copyright page.

LIBRARY OF CONGRESS CATALOGING IN PUBLICATION DATA
Buchsbaum, Julianne.
The apothecary's heir / Julianne Buchsbaum.
p. cm. — (National poetry series)
Poems.
ISBN 978-0-14-312141-1
I. Title.
PS3602.U26A66 2012
811'.6—dc23   2012004844

Printed in the United States of America
Set in Simoncini Garamond Std
Designed by Ginger Legato

ALWAYS LEARNING   PEARSON

In memory of my father,
Herbert J. Buchsbaum, 1934–1989

ACKNOWLEDGMENTS

I would like to express my gratitude to the friends who have taken the time to engage with the poems in this book—especially Jerry Masinton, Lynne McMahon, Sherod Santos, John Estes, Carolina Ebeid, and Jeffrey Pethybridge. I would also like to thank my mother for the faith she has had in my work, for her boundless generosity of spirit, and for all of her support throughout the years.

Many thanks to the editors of the journals in which these poems first appeared:

"The Day After" and "The Weeds of Walker's Point," *Blue Island Review*

"First Love," *Southwest Review*

"The Making of the English Working Class," *Catch Up*

"Last Night I Felt the Need to Write to You" and "Seven Views of Longboat Key, Florida," *New Orleans Review*

"Fata Morgana," *The Journal*

"The Mad Dream of Sea-Things in the Bay of Bengal," *The Iowa Review*

"Summer of Fires" and "A Death in the Snow," *Columbia: A Journal of Literature and Art*

"Still Life with Rooms People Live In," *Phoebe*

"With Venom and Wonder" [titled "This Wanton Geometry"], *Guernica*

CONTENTS

I.

II.

III.

THE APOTHECARY'S HEIR

I.

The Making of the English Working Class

I.

I thought my brother would be among the monks
left over in this world. With the shiny pallor

of a just-painted still life, he was good at keeping
quiet, warding off the sallies of someone strong.

It was mortifying, the mementos of his own
ascesis piled in little heaps inside his room,

relics of the kind of body that can go a long time
without sleep or food. He told me it was love

that made the world go round. Our mother
was a nun to him in her spotless cotton shirts.

She never cooked. Sometimes I am numb
to the world's noise. And when we went

to temple, people sat in the pews like they were
at the movies; it made no difference to them.

My body was there, but my mind was elsewhere,
wandering through wealds where lives were virginal

and wild, wondering about the bodies of ancient
queens and where they were buried, maybe on beaches

where I wrote my name, improvident, and hoped
to be seen. If not now, in some other, quieter time.

II.

Have you ever loved so much the truth of your own
death came home to you? In Manchester, 1833,

half of the children born to spinners died. The pelvic
bones of girls who worked in the mills could not make room

for the new life coming through. Children given
dirty rags to suck were dying from disease.

It's possible to die from not being touched—no one
knew that then—and the monks were not to be disturbed

in their dark adorations, their ancient formulas
for making something potent go away, be quiet, good.

Sometimes I sing when I've light,
but not in the dark; I dare not sing then.

III.

When a child's skin is translucent, people think
he could be anything. I am learning even now

that this is not the case. Even when a page
is blank, certain things can and can't be said.

My father was safe in his hospital lab, studying cells
gone awry in bodies and how to kill them off.

My brother taught me young that night is the womb
of nothing human. Over the beaches of the Queen of Carthage,

the sky must have been like a face with its features
rubbed out. If I keep my head down long enough,

I'll be there, in my long-standing withdrawal from
the present moment. And like the remnants

of an ancient still life, the stars still look at us,
safe in their monadic, monastic, inscrutable rites.

Ars Poetica

The desk gleams at me every day with
the merciless sheen of an operating table.
Where is the needle, the ligature fine enough
to stitch the wound between word and thing?

Where is the chloroform to knock this subject out?
I mutter lines like the Hippocratic oath.
My family wonders why I'm so preoccupied.
My shift never ends. I'm always on call.

Rough drafts pile up on the filing cabinet
like former patients leering in an endless
convalescence, smelling of glue and Wite-Out;
they hint at missed deadlines, malpractice suits.

Am I the surgeon to suture such a gaping?
I disinfect my scalpels in the autoclave
of solitude; the room reeks of phenol—
but hygiene is not enough. Errors spawn

like pathogens. Nor am I a faith healer.
Praying is as obsolete as mustard plasters.
Let the squeamish keep their lab coats clean.
I mask my face and swab at the blood-leaks.

Confession

I was an arrant antisocial
in among the evergreens or

sitting with my back straight
in the library, studying for hours.

I wanted all A's, wanted to be God,
come with grappling hooks and a pistol

to found nations, then fleece them.
My homeroom teacher was

my idol, and my heart dropped.
Trees were given every utopia

and epilogue of honor.
Sit, she said, *and convey to me*

your nights. Sit like that.
Stones froze in place, me hunching

with serious doubts at her shrine.
Damn the evergreens, she said,

in my backyard where I confessed
(rhetoric wouldn't let me rest)

to a corrupted phonology. Proust
came anyway to delete all this with

a monocle. She was the trees in me,
rural and conflicted, at the parade

of nations. Either way I minded her
going. I erased it from my mind and

all night I pored over Proust, deepening
my dependency on his books, looking

for wordstations to reside in.
Then, I was quiet and the trees had a new

ontology. I sat before word-mirrors.
She became a pastoral homeland

I laid waste to with fissures, doubts, and
phone calls. Back from the woods

recently, she comes with a lusty rhythm
and Latinate words. (She fails to phone me,

then sends flowers.) I confess evil
thoughts, end up exhausted. When I

express myself, my tryings harden
the darkness. I believe I was born to this.

And My Clothing Shall Be Cruelty

I am a nerve laid bare in bald light.
All night monks howled in my head,

tearing their robes; musty as winding-sheets,
they came apart easily. I turn from

the bad news hatching in my head,
the gravestone gospel. I have turned

all my flower girls to Giftmädchen.
The world rots at its root: it is spring.

The parks pullulate with germs, larvae;
the sapsucker taps the thawed resin.

I am a crooked root in a throne of gold,
mouthing my ex cathedras. I have trapped

my appetites in lobster cages: sometimes
a fat red claw rattles the locked bars

and I dunk them further in icy blue.
My hands claw the armrests of my chair.

I touch what I touch with a violence, as if
to stop the subatomic flux, the knifing rains.

The Ruined Circus of Eros

Flesh whose tenuous illness seems
unjust, you follow the owl's

hollow-boned prestissimo.
Its tune wrung out of wet air.

Meanwhile, the corroding ocher
of the slag heap seethes.

Freighters accelerate from the port.
Something gross inheres in the hog lot.

Bird-notes inert in the sweet
gum trees nurture benediction.

I do not trust my inner child.
I do not trust my tutor.

Like ruptured caryatids
who can no longer carry

the neoclassical, these trees
bear up under the quotidian.

First Love

There is no Daphne there, though I can see
in the tree's pained angles its stance of *I*
will go no farther, leave me be, its pose
of not-to-be-violated calm. And I, wooing it
with eyes and words, bring forth nothing
but its frozen ghost, its starved-down shadow
dying even as I put it into words;
I who am no Apollo, unbalanced, without
aplomb, despite this sun that dilates
and cracks apart, rives and unsheathes,
lays the rough bark of that stubborn tree
starkly open to me—even then it escapes,
makes off with its nymph-hair, twigs
of brushed gold streaming in wind, it flees
and I follow. Why these few shrunken leaves
flapping like feeble pulses? This up-forking,
torqued mass defoliated, intertwined,
reigning in the backyard like an antlered divine?
Dappled with lichen, white spots like spittle,
rivulets of gritty shadow on the bark,
the tree, like a great wooden mind
through which a squirrel dashes like
an afterthought, never talks back to me.

Leaf-Mutterings

Without the violets, you could walk
into winter without holding your breath.
Without opening the door, you could step
into tents that summer makes in the leaves.
Summer comes in sighs wrapped in sheets
of violet. The songs you hold on to are *Jaybird
Wing on the Lawn, Lilies Awake in the Wind,*
and *Portents of Snow.* There must be some
summer nights you remember. The leafsoul
is asleep in the cold. Is anything left alive in
these spheres? Without the leafsoul, you had
to discard what you'd thought of as life.
Asleep in its habitat of song, the leafsoul
is chanting something lovely or slovenly.
It has no handmaiden nor midwife. The minutes,
the hours, the days are like jackets it wears
on its way to the castle. It sleeps in a tent
of rejected leaves. The leafsoul dreams
of the sea and those who sigh for the sea.

Seven Views of Longboat Key, Florida

**

The sound of wharves aswarm
with rats woke me from stupor

to nuance of anemone
and blackfin, a world come

dripping from distant isles,
lavish with lime trees.

Some eyes see sky,
some eyes see heaven.

**

A quell of gull and wave,

a final phylum, an *untergehen*,
it stuns like a drug,

a waterlogged god, oblivious
as Porifera waving in the abyss—

huge, indifferent, hoodlum.
Fishermen ply it like an annus

mirabilis, a secret death wish.

**

My canvas fills with a false paradise.
I have not seen the sea at all today.

Barnacles, blue waves, dank
fumes from moldy gangplanks.

A month of debaucheries dies in my mouth
as waves compose their rags of blue.

They answer me with motley shells,
corbeils of foam like flowers of hell.

**

It smells bereft.

It smells of underleaf.

**

A school of mackerel
translated into gore
by the gearwheels
of an ocean liner.

**

Amid the bric-a-brac *v' yitkadash*
of Florida, these leaves look like katydids

cooked in lukewarm bile, but gnarled
and dry as the claws of the turkey buzzard

camouflaged in the detritus of dying
palm trees behind the new gas station.

They feel like nylon stockings
bunched in a drawer for months on end.

Flame-colored motorcycles roar
down the boulevard not far from here.

**

At odds with everyone,

I idealize the island,

its narcotic solitude.

Alien where

fungus grows drunkenly,

I'm about to become

one to come home to.

Eve of Darkness

The lines are down; it will soon be night.
A night interrupted by bird-cackles like ladders

leading down to damp caves. A night of green
liquids spilled from glass vials outside a motel.

And if, on the eve of darkness, there is no boy
nor stable self nor horse in the snarled leaves

below rational inquiry, you will look at yourself—

you who stand alone in the stains of a night
that increases in star noise like the memos

of an old hegemony, in the impossible museums
where all the cold statues do no blossoming,

where gigantic hungers of carnivores are canceled,
and you will create out of that timeless, erratic

capital a little shattered moment for which
night is the only rightful heir and apothecary.

The Workers

The tedium of their desk sets is endless,
and the crux of every living thing offends them.

Clients come to make oblations in the cubicles
where oblivion is dictated in creepy syllables.

They gesture opaquely, starry-eyed, whitening
their cuffs with tiny toxic ministrations of bleach.

Hollow bones in wrinkle-free pants.
Having surrendered themselves to calendars

and chemical fumes, meticulously, all day long,
they loosen death from the diagrams of paradise.

Soon they will take possession of stale doughnuts,
dried-out azaleas, and ride home in black cars

or enter barrooms in red scarves. Long after
they've left the building to a plastic silence,

the receptionist will feign indifference while
vacuums unleash electrified whispers of disgust.

Postindustrial Sublime

November, and not for the first time: a subdued,
ocherous light from trees where a crow, imperious
and dour, is like a black-turbaned sultan presiding
over blended valences of light. Steel brackets
block out the Ethereal in the city where you come
to adumbrate the ways the Real vaporizes the Ideal
in its medullary rays. November, and an ocherous light
subjects the sunken trees to a truce. November,
and for the time being light subordinates the live oaks
to the bleak operations of crows stirring in the branches.
Blundering out of a stalemate with meaninglessness,
the damned extract themselves from fragments
and redesign the architecture of their lives while fresh
shreds of trash collect beneath pylons by the river.
I would spare you the gridiron sublime of a world
depleted of carnivals while death moves its tongue
over the city where words do not hold the world in place,
this place of beginnings of fragments of words
that sound like someone trying to suppress a scream.

With Venom and Wonder

Midnights, beyond the fjords, widowed from timbers,
I hear, in drowned valleys or barges off the coast of Maine,
a retinue of echoes—*Nadine, Dwight, Tyrone and the Golden
Boys*—above a graveyard of cars, stars fall into the fat

green hills where I watch you leave your wildness behind—
I wanna send this one out to you—while you sleep
and the women come toward you with their beauty and
their mouthfuls of earth, goblets of milk on silver trays

like Mary's or Semele's—you've seen such monotints
in moons and dreams of moons, marl of palsied trees,
Lone Wolf, Nashville Kid, but never thought to take
such cold inside and make it yours, wind like a mongrel dog

snarling across the fields outside the ranch your parents
bought in '89, in fits of sunlight flecked like *Little Lyle,
all those wild dogs out there,* fronds like day laborers
bowed in the scrivening breezes, sleep a kind of bag

you fall into at night where all the women wear hats
covered in money, dust-colored wings of moths, and other
soft insects, where *all our friends out in the Ninth Ward*
talk of how to migrate beyond the farthest shore of Florida,

with nothing but dropped consonants and a lessened luster
of matted hair—of how, in the nounstillness of the sea,
a monkfish steals under stars—and still, in the Prussian
blue bluffs of summer, this wanton geography of love remains.

The Weeds of Walker's Point

We take turns behind the gas station where
the weeds of Walker's Point give up their green.
Now, in the cashmere sky, a moth-eaten hole is
the gibbous moon that hangs over a statue
of Solomon Juneau. Suddenly the air is aromatic
of weapons, silver badges, as squad cars multiply
around a Plymouth like dime-store cigars.
A dead zone engenders another kind of architecture
while the boys of Milwaukee ride through the night
in taxis, and the night is violins, laudanum,
wires bringing oblivion to all your fears
drowned in old scrollwork, valerian drops,
a light touch of rot, the junkyard's deepest slumber.
Snarling, grunting, someone pushes a stalled car
in the rain. A figure slowly wheels himself through
a parking lot. The blurred scene sinks down like
a train wreck in the distance. Stars proliferate
like disco balls spitting out bits of capitalism.

Fata Morgana

Dark as sloe: excoriations
of shadows from the thorny
canopy. Night moves on.

You wait for winter.

Air crusted with leaves and
corpus of pine needles shifting.

Furthermore, dapple-lobed
oak leaves, matrix of mist.

That tree pirates your light,
its branch deranging the air.

Flies burgeon in this broth
of gold light. Know
she is near you, that shadows

breed in the cut places
as you watch. Pale blue
phlox, bloodroot reticulum.

Ulcers of light eat gobbets of dark.

Mist smothers the air
where small mammals loosen
her pine-colored hair.

Summer of Fires

I.

Season of third-degree burns and third-rate
thoughts, stasis is a place where stars go
black, a football stadium filled with dead
leaves. Stasis is a place of pale flowers
behind parking lots. Season of rags,
mustard gas, and Mausers, I'm putting
you to sleep in my arms with some opium,
you constellation of germs and viruses,
as an animal dies in a vacant lot and wind
chafes the carapace of this tank town,
its muscle cars up on blocks in the yards.

II.

Damp mother lode of pathogens and mold,
to annotate with wounds, and yet more wounds,
the body of a child, what power broker
or precinct captain would not muscle you
into a smoke-filled room to watch you gnash
your teeth and murmur of corruption?
Season of frogs and fecundity, bring on
more, and always more, bee-harassed
flowers. The mockingbird that died under
the bush will continue to infect the night
with incoherent bristles of its wings.

III.

Season of fog and narrow boxes for still-
borns, paint those cherry trees with fungus
till the whole sick harvest splashes down
like a carpet bomb. Always budding silently
behind the beehive's humid cells, ripe
with apple cores and peach pits, marrow
of hazelnuts and bones, musty death shifts
the body rapidly between parentheses.
Wind separates the vapors of poppy blooms.
In this drugged state after a painful operation,
I want to stay with you forever, undisturbed.

Leaflet

I fed a little light to the industrial trestle.
I threw a few rocks at the exit sign.

I dallied among drainage pipes
and clattered in a cart of hemlocks.

I raked a damp path in a ditch.
I ramped up the currents on the pain

machine until August rode in
on a red wind and some dust.

I ventured out into the corn to look
for my dog. I took steps to distance

myself from goodness. Loaded it above
the sluice gate, graveyard, pavement.

Letter from the Edge

Dear blackout, dear god-mouth, you creak
like an old robot in your riot gear.

My insurgencies, sir, against your gloved hands
and manhandling are worse than you imagine.

Hat brim low, wearing dark clothes,
you are a man of ice proliferating lies.

Sir, for every lost soul there comes a lull.
Be still on your horse, sir—your bullies

are dead now or bankrupt in blue hills
spotted with horses no nostalgia corrupts.

And who is lord, sir, of these dogs that paw
at yesterday's quarry, clawed open?

They hulk by the pines as if waiting
to enter a room where someone is dying.

The Day After

The violets are washed jewels in the yard.
When she wakes, she does not cry.

She watches the clock steadily.
Leaf-newts darken in small bunches

that morning draws apart at six a.m.
The held breath is of God, she thinks.

Feathers brush against buckles
like precepts vaguely remembered,

and the sky is a binary of bird and no-bird,
a conjunction of buntings and nothing.

She would like to go inside the minds of lions,
behind their jeweled and godless eyes.

The day is merely a collection of objects
without color and colors without edges

as the north wind bleeds into the gums
of cattle standing in a patch of iron rain.

A Death in the Snow

Epitaphs covered with mold,
black markets of jimsonweeds—

from a shadow this pine
will bury back in the earth,

I return to a stockyard of broken veins
near the cornfields where

a scarecrow shuffles its cuffs of straw.
Deer bend their heads to a lie

that dies near a woodpile—
my dear one, my child.

The dead lie in asocial scatterings
in the rustling gothic *Ehebruch*

of dusk. A dog, stirred from its daze
by the rustle of creatures clearing a log,

bares its teeth at what is left
of the earth piled up next to

the small dirty palace of a birdhouse.
Cold as an antiquarian plow in the snow,

I return to the woods and leave behind
my list of things to do, leave it lying

in the snow like an ice pack for
a wound, where the dead lie taciturn

and hoodless and hived in the loaded soil.

Notes Toward a Patchboard Mechanics

Cogwheels spinning in the factory's gut,
anchored in green air near the steel panopticon—

blanched worm gears of death turn around
each hour siphoned off so cruelly.

Meanwhile, scurf shed by the lathe
curls in soft piles. Anvils lack blacksmiths.

But who is taskmaster of torches,
of this obtuse toil without an oracle?

The stars suggest a kind of death
in the far-off scattered light they send.

My words are coiled in fiberglass threads
that network out across the city.

I lounge beneath a Bakelite sky,
delirious at each pneumatic clamp

with which I seem to grasp the truth.
Here in the wind, my heart is isinglass

below joists that perform
like giant strongmen in seared air.

At the Syllable Sale

At the syllable sale: a tiny loom, a Latin noun.
It is a gold noun, a ghost town, a deathkit held

under a peasant's lick of standing water.
Wholesale syllables go for the minimum but

may be disfigured. Time blooms like a slow
flower in hot July. At the syllable sale,

some are ruined kings or hapless crones.
At the syllable sale, time holds still in the poppy

flowers. The word *idle* waits for me
by the wastebasket. At the syllable sale, time

has a blood transfusion; the words worry me,
all the weird terminologies. With a small fist

of syllables, heading for home, I must admit
that the language I know does not know me.

In the Beautiful, Long-Gone, and Godless Season of Hereafter

Return to razed fields: dull shocks of corn
in mutilated rows, hosts to locusts, grass
snakes, grubs. Harvest's end: hatchets
splintering late fruit fallen to rot and be
ravaged along the hoar and hairless
curvature of the earth's spine. Dogwoods
doomed by dark nests, fungus, crows like
black flames with forked wings. Ghost-
colored but not yet dead, neighbors turn
to stare with glassy eyes. Not yet beneath
the earthy kiss of chisels on stone, parts
of the Pentateuch spoken in a stony tongue,
you are *tertium quid* to the dichotomies
in question. Train whistles bring you back
to how cold you are in the windstorm.
Train tracks portion off this rain-ruined
place: sallow as a brass lamp snuffed
in the dark, the sky is no consolation.
Like a bride trundled off, eyes shut tight,
to a saltbox home in the heartland—still
enshrined, like something carved of wood
and set on fire, alone in the scarecrow fields—
you wait and are willing.

I Wanted More

The tree spurts Listerine-
yellow curlicues of leaves.

All the way from Rock Bridge
to here, I smelled the fallen

musk of its summergrowth.
Crosshatched by catclaws, frost-

blanched, pocked with moss,
and marred by woodpecker beaks,

sunscald, and its own aborted
growth spurts, this enormous

digester of bad air and bird parts
itches itself against a breeze

that builds to a low howling
whir in a minor key.

Moist breeze, come not unto me.
I wanted more than these

night-aborted birdsongs:
torrid affairs in a suburban abyss,

distorted ghosts, Goths in rehab,
cardboard torsos, dethroned gods.

Tell me I should level with these
low, warty, dendriform shapes

in the grass. The pungent
Dumpster-smell of dead dreams.

I fold my hands in this leaf-light,
this green nowhere-rain,

an enormous lore collapsing
in moss-colored air.

Infant Dusk

What I dream makes me sad
and wed to secrecy.

I walked into the woods
with a disposable camera.

A kind of calamity led me
to an antechamber

of ruinous dusk, a hermitage
where I fit myself for dying.

I have erred, infected slavery's
secret heaven. I brood about

some sickly moonbeam breaking
upon a murderer's face.

Behind the small wheels of a hurt
smile, an altar boy freezes.

He long ago passed through the Pastoral.
His words begin with bitterness.

Soul-compelling thought growing
upon a grave, come hither, master

the world inside me. I am an open
phoneme, an infant dusk

that daylight has bled out of.

The Mad Dream of Sea-Things in the Bay of Bengal

Seagull beaks. Spoilation.
Off the bay, bowsprit fractures,

bent moon silvering the cracks.
Clouds that open like crab claws.

Dismembering waves, maimed limbs.
Smell of citron in city markets.

Quays, crows, cockleshells.
Dead men's fingers that wash ashore,

clutch seaweed shreds, have
no homecoming. The icy undertow

that dines on salted seabird bones.
Moonglint that makes of the sea

a broken machine, adagios of whale,
virgin tides of hoary brine and many-

fathoms-down stony madrepore.
Green-marbled depths, fatal nadir,

octopod and pirates, cold head-
quarters of kraken, dead calm.

Highland Park, 2004

Behind the trash-littered bulwark of a dead
trailer park: a dingy dog licks an empty
wrapper, and love for the ne'er-do-wells
down by the pool hall turns as sour as
a baseball hat worn backward.
I'm tired of the cold, empty streets
with their thin black dogs. *Nowhere,*
a mother's long, didactic finger wags.
*You'll get nowhere with that kind
of attitude.* Mother can shake her finger
all she wants. I scatter my attitude
everywhere, and it sucks. At the local
drive-in downtown, a cash-poor carhop
leans into the dashboard of a cop car,
saying, *I'm parched.* In this neighborhood,
the old ladies sit on their porches all day long,
broochless, wearing wigs, playing cards,
as rubbish swells in back alleys like
litanies from the local Bible-thumper.
Meanwhile, underneath the chassis
of a dilapidated Chevrolet, globular
clusters of oily beads seem to grow
upward from the concrete, and I am far
from home, in some other zone, watching
a small bird hop brokenly outside
an abandoned storefront mall. A mild
seasickness washes over me as I look up
at the sweet toxic green of the sky
in which the moon will soon be a broken
rhinestone skull among the star swarms.

Deep in the Sabbath Dusk

I.

I abide where all the minds are colonized
by microchips. God is not awake

in these arrangements of razor wire.
Something sacred was erased by the radars.

II.

One fingernail of criticism
comes between the world as it is

and the world as I see it. A flag jerks
in the wind like someone else's skin.

III.

Deep in the Sabbath dusk, the nation
founders on the fake brown foliage

of its fast-food restaurants.
With a wave of my Visa,

my internal hell
grows total and solar.

I can't be this person anymore.

IV.

The young men will not wait
past midnight on the blankets,

snuffing out their lust with pharmaceuticals.
I am merely another animal down

where the trailer courts give themselves
up to the night and the cows lie down in alfalfa.

V.

Someday the water will come again,
sheets of rain slanting like a damnation,

clouds like a pollution of mind.
Someday our parallel shapes will stop

moving. As I said, we are three parts
Being, three parts Becoming.

I never meant to do you wrong.

III.

Still Life with Rooms People Live In

I.

Another squat, windowless morning
murmurs on its industrial hook.

Outside, the moon is a flatbed truck
filled with the leftover ice of night,

and alder trees keep going nowhere,
dressed in droplets, globes of scum.

Our daily menu begins crushing out
bomb shelters, electric blankets.

Waiting for your hands, morning spits
me out over cratered staple factories,

poisoned black clouds. Waiting for your
hands: two birds going nowhere, dressed

in tin—they know so well how to sleep.

II.

Lampposts, silhouetted in amber shafts,
slowly begin to rust. So very slowly,

the nurse I love begins to withdraw her offer
of foghorns, seafoam, mentholated pine.

I don't care, don't care how quickly
the star-eaten machinery of these South

Chicago steel mills disappears. The bridge
between us is an x'ed-out exhaust fume.

Faintly, nursed by hard plastic,
your sickbed genuflections reach me

unripened. When you bend to read it,
your daily menu darkens quietly

as alder trees gather power in the rain.

III.

Night, grotesque, organic, unfolds
into the palm of a dropped puppet.

It's Friday evening, and the future is
again a faceless nurse who withdraws

when I rise to take what she offers.
Men curse the bad angles of broken

machines, bleed droplets in arcs
of carbon residue. I have no idea

how to sleep, how boarded-up bomb
shelters gather power in the rain.

We live in a room where, so very
slowly, my finger to your lips,

you suffer the distance between us.

Ode on a Mode of Lethe

A mode of Lethe washes over me,
engorging me with feelings for lyric
poetry. It's like a nightingale trapped
in a sewage pipe, struggling to get free.

Meanwhile, deep in the Black Forest,
there is medicine for metaphysicians
where flies commune over atrophied violets.
There, the antiseptic darkness preserves

the fruit trees, the candy-colored flowers,
and the wherewithal of each wild summer
month in which I softly name my love
and ponder death in difficult rhymes.

In darkness embalmed with the smell of exhaust
fumes and chemicals, there is the softer smell
of turbines. O, for a cup completely full of the sun.
The thought that I could drink it inside
the visible world leaves me weak in the knees.

The colors of summer numbly become
those of fall. The sun discards its happy
verbs behind in the veins of all the leaves.
But your excessive happiness annoys me,
bird, plotting to flee from all this umbrage.

I Prefer the Ebb Tide

I cannot name
this place ushered in

by hanging tags and paid tolls.
Yesterday disintegrates

in gold-plated bracts
and pieces of cartilage.

Under the tinselly prayers
of workmen, I pause,

agape at the black aspen
by the watercourse.

Blind stars fly up into
the spoiled milk of the sky.

In this religion of cold lights
and steel girders, all night long

I pause at rest-stops on the way
to somewhere more colorful

and lit up. The sky emptied
of God is old bone, obsidian.

Death turns blue in the aspens.
I prefer the ebb tide

with its luckless, quieted phylum
of washed-up invertebrates

to the impertinent metal
clacking of these oily rails.

Last Night I Felt the Need to Write to You

I doubt if it would change your mind, but what is destroyed
below rigid alignments of bent tree-crowns will someday
furl upward toward the sun, even in glacial air. So many icy
suggestions of things unborn and unwished for recede
under frost's lost and forgotten palaces while one lone bird
flies beyond these white-ridged distances. *Six months seems
like a really long time.* And yet the ice, in its frail approximations
of dead nodes, its quietus under the descending matrix of frost,
seems to be the source of everything that's been detached
phlegmatically from the trees. *I don't want to be unreasonable.*
And I, finally, detach myself from these forms of dead
or dying starlife, these thoughts of you, the infolding
they achieve under the glass mouths of god-forms advancing
quietly. *I doubt if it would change your mind.* All these squelched
beings receding into spiral self-opposed universes of notched
intaglios. *I suppose it's fruitless to try to convince you.*
In these blades going down to the blotched bronze earth,
there is this thing, like starlife, *caught between us.*

Minister of Leaves

I awaken to afternoon's ornamented grave.
Moss welcomes my sky, seems to lie split
and hacked. Here where the day is
a deadened blade, cables carve the sky
outside while the city's demolished
buildings sink into an iron sleep. No daybreak
cold reminder of the gull's wing, whose
falling off is a white noise implicit
in the subway's silver speed. On back roads,
the world swerves in a ditch, seizes up
and lets go a bag marked BIOHAZARD.
See the sun enclosed in low, chopped clouds.
Alone with my own name, I know blue rain.
Squat purple earth. White trees steady me.

Sequined and Sinister

Traveler among rheumy and teratoid
glooms, purchaser of rank farm goods,

you, far away from here, beneath
a milk-blue sky, have the porcelained

aura of the untouched-by-misery.
Like some gravel-dredger of unlit depths,

who, wallowing, will drown
too soon, you go with a tiny flare-light

of vitriol into starlit tellurian places.
Of weed-stems in an empty lot

that opens onto a lumber mill
where nobody goes all summer,

you report in whispers behind crates
of fruit rinds, palsied in a crepe-paper dawn.

Lakeshore Hospital, 1987: A Dialogue of Self and Soul

Orderlies hand out meds in Dixie cups
and warm whole milk for tryptophan.
Nights now, I never possess you entirely.
In bed by eight each night, we dream
of nurses with ice cubes for eyes as
shadows spin carousels along the walls.
Correctly jointed, you are a mouth of death.
Our faces pale as fog blown in from filthy harbors,
we stare at bolted window screens while
down the hall post-lobotomies drift in gentle
Lethe-dreams, slow as floating jellyfish.
I swear I will not burn for you or anyone.
We lie on the floor as a bearded man
intones some vapid words into our ears.
I'll never catch up to you now.
We try to picture "somewhere nice." Later,
a boy is talking to an empty chair; he thinks
he sees his father there. *Love is an infection.*
A code red blares from intercoms, and in
the Quiet Room a dose of Thorazine glistens
in a thin syringe. *The hands of our fathers
fasten upon us.* At lunch we eat from plastic trays
with plastic forks and spoons. *The whites
of your eyes are weedy and ahistorical.*
We've made a mess of us. They will not
let us, will not let us make a mess again.

Three Brief Meditations on Oak Trees

I.

Nothing at the gates of my thoughts
but the old, decayed face of the sun,
a valet to usher me into the depths
of these old stumps. Voyager through
pale, annulled provinces, I come to know
snowy quadrants of a wood-block world.
Mist glues these twigs into an opaque beauty.
Lexicographer of decay, I love the briny
lowercase letters of the snow, the bouquets
of rotting vegetation in a clump of mud.

II.

What icy lobes will siphon off the self-
opposed *ding an sich* of suckled rhizomes?
This late-winter landscape falls as a surplus
on these husks and shadow-blades, finally
nursed into being by this light. I am here
as though there is a thing to see, a tree-thing,
around which everything else gathers like
a panoply. Walking quietly past some black
liquid pooling in polygons in someone's yard,
feeling the day's jagged, swift destructions
coming down, I confront an austerity
in which dies a small part of my inner self.

III.

As though it has chewed through the table
of elements to be here, the world sponged clear
of snow is swart beneath attenuated twigs.
I forsake the knowing mind and make for
a quietus in which the world is contained
in one dying oak. Suckled in this icy breast,
what is there to love but lobes of shadow?
The corpus of this one tree, its tendrils velvety
as licked fur. Split-open husk of the world
drizzled by the brass-colored creek-bed.
These are the final profusions of winter
flung out among the vanishings.

Say the Sea, Then

I.

Say the sea, then, this gray suspension,
this great abolition, or alibi—

pale hands dig out its gels,
its sorbet-colored fish. Burned by its surfaces,

bald people put on dark sunglasses.
They gather its slimy pastilles

as the sea crawls off
with a brief whistle of affliction.

II.

Is this the sea, then, this strange revision
of people, places, and things?

This garish, this gaudy conversation
piece without philosophy?

A green tide pool opens its eye,
fat with swallowed images.

Behind the commodities of the boardwalk,
tall weeds tremble like last week's classifieds.

III.

This great retirement of the piebald
and anachronistic is the sea.

Why is it so calm here? Where is the one
who hides? Proprietors of elastic fixtures

come here, surrounded by gatherers
of shells or quiet sounds of the sea.

Remember these salty waves,
how they waste entire Sundays, smilingly.

For Most of My Life, This Was Never My Life

Odd how you sent me postcards of weather reports
and the verdant and basic darkness of your face.

They put lanterns inside to detect which one is
wounded where. The weather is mustard-gas,

morbidezza fog, a downpour of fever through
a hole in Utopia. Further on in the fairgrounds,

birds defile the air with cries that sound like *delete*
delete. The roads zigzag up to the old stadium,

the boarded-up theater. You can't sleep enough
in this weather, surrounded by electric fences,

dreaming of digits and Sputniks. Streets deserted
beneath the incandescence of floodlights. Further on

in the industrial tracts, my favorite river-watching spot,
a dampness darkens. *I offer you a fabrication of myself*

broken-winded in a wicker chair. Always the Mississippi
moving on, leaving me with nothing but the flawed

flatbed of the future tense. I am far from home, and
the sky throws nothing back but that bird-in-flight blue,

like a huge mistake the sun hatched in its solitude.
I'm not scared, you said, *of touching your changing face.*

One Last Daystar Fades

One last daystar fades
on a breeze of novocaine.
Sun-dabbled plaster garden
gnomes keep watch
in a sludge of honeysuckle.

I drink from delicate alembics
until the mauled replicas
of nightbeasts no longer
frighten me. I bought them
from nameless storefront idlers,

disheveled apparitions
on cobblestone streets,
the palsied hand of an old
apothecary standing
like a disjointed mannequin,

his ink-black silhouette
a wild-looking prefiguration
of suffering, a tattered
and malefic one presiding
over cool bottles of multicolored pills.

I pass fields of feeding bovines
in a fractured twilight
littered with rusty sewer lids,
where phosphorous night-lights
wink from behind a briar bush.

Leaves Crinkle in the Woods

Leaves crinkle in the woods like people telling secrets.
I walk on them with featherweight steps, like a person
canceling her own commitments. Deep in the warehouse,
someone begins dispelling lies. Something keeps shutting
down the musculature of night animals. There is no
remedy for this difficult day. The sky has thrice turned
to acetate now over Rollins Avenue. Beetles crawl
into the gutter like students of what is down there.
My sisters surround me and allay my fears. I fear I have
no sisters, or if I had, I have driven them away.
We were wandering once through the streets
of Chicago with music in our ears. We found everything
mislabeled and metaphysical. My sisters listen to me
for hours in the dark every night, their hands resting
lightly in their laps. When I bring them the dead wine
of my memories, they drink it and are bird-eyed.

Prayer from Port Neches

Algal facade of swaybacked warehouses,
empty plywood churches, a gnashing sound
from scrabbled pews: *Dear God, please*
help me out of this. Scripted fricatives
from the long-winded lung of the inner city.
A breakdown of vine clusters
in the weather-cracked switching yards,
the moon staring down like a catatonic derelict.
Dear Lord, please help me survive.
I keep thinking there must be something
manifold in the barren moonfields,
must be something beyond this inhuman
wind in the scrub brush, the fluke
of morningfog over the harbor.
I have this fear, dear Lord, that will not subside,
that we will not survive. Tattered pariahs
come from a clogged and bluish otherworld,
lean-boned in a cloud of diesel smoke.
All day I keep my head down at work and try
to be mindless. *Lord, help me to get by.*

Lament of the Hunger Artist

Dolefully, an odd discoverer, I ramble down
deserted streets inspecting the sullen houses
that make even gold light rot on their roofs.
I did not come to catechize among the palms of midnight
nor expand upon the savagery of winter's cruciforms.
Did not come to parlay a leaf-shorn nothingness against
cadaverous refuges of noon. All day, I push sheets
of paper around in a room. I do not carry certain parts
of myself into conversation. I steer clear of conversation.
Noon scented with blooms breeds a bareness of yellow,
melted metals, broken locusts. Did not come
to trace the purple trees with quills or brushes.
So much for the flitter of a few starved leaves.
Annotator of tattered nests, connoisseur of clouds,
I leave behind the flaws of many strange places.
Midday comes with its criticisms and an abundance
of blank labels. Did not come to flatter, did not come
to pray. Amid these branches intertwined like bronze
conduits and the late-afternoon opulence of plaster
facades, successive shadows make mystical harbor.

NOTES

"The Making of the English Working Class": The title of the poem and the italicized lines at the end of the second section come from E. P. Thompson's book *The Making of the English Working Class*.

"And My Clothing Shall Be Cruelty": The title of this poem is based on a line from William Blake's poem *Milton*, plate 18, line 20. The poem itself was inspired by Francis Bacon's painting *Study after Velázquez's Portrait of Pope Innocent X*.

"With Venom and Wonder": The phrase "with venom and wonder" was taken from the liner notes to Bob Dylan's 1976 album *Desire*: "Where do I begin . . . on the heels of Rimbaud moving like a dancing bullet thru the secret streets of a hot New Jersey night filled with venom and wonder." The lines in italics are from *Down by Law*, the 1986 film by Jim Jarmusch. The phrase "like Mary's or Semele's" is a line from "Fire-Eater" by Ted Hughes.

PENGUIN POETS